THE SURVEY KIT

Purpose: The purposes of this 9-volume Kit are to enable readers to prepare and conduct surveys and become better users of survey results. Surveys are conducted to collect information by asking questions of people on the telephone, face-to-face, and by mail. The questions can be about attitudes, beliefs, and behavior as well as socioeconomic and health status. To do a good survey also means knowing how to ask questions, design the survey (research) project, sample respondents, collect reliable and valid information, and analyze and report the results. You also need to know how to plan and budget for your survey.

Users: The Kit is for students in undergraduate and graduate classes in the social and health sciences and for individuals in the public and private sectors who are responsible for conducting and using surveys. Its primary goal is to enable users to prepare surveys and collect data that are accurate and useful for primarily practical purposes. Sometimes, these practical purposes overlap the objectives of scientific research, and so survey researchers will also find the Kit useful.

Format of the Kit: All books in the series contain instructional objectives, exercises and answers, examples of surveys in use and illustrations of survey questions, guidelines for action, checklists of do's and don'ts, and annotated references.

Volumes in The Survey Kit:

1. **The Survey Handbook**
   Arlene Fink

2. **How to Ask Survey Questions**
   Arlene Fink

3. **How to Conduct Self-Administered and Mail Surveys**
   Linda B. Bourque and *Eve P. Fielder*

4. **How to Conduct Interviews by Telephone and in Person**
   James H. Frey and *Sabine Mertens Oishi*

5. **How to Design Surveys**
   Arlene Fink

6. **How to Sample in Surveys**
   Arlene Fink

7. **How to Measure Survey Reliability and Validity**
   Mark S. Litwin

8. **How to Analyze Survey Data**
   Arlene Fink

9. **How to Report on Surveys**
   Arlene Fink

THE SURVEY KIT

TSK 8

HOW TO
ANALYZE
SURVEY DATA

ARLENE FINK

SAGE Publications
International Educational and Professional Publisher
Thousand Oaks   London   New Delhi

For information address:

 SAGE Publications, Inc.
2455 Teller Road
Thousand Oaks, California 91320
E-mail: order@sagepub.com

SAGE Publications Ltd.
6 Bonhill Street
London EC2A 4PU
United Kingdom

SAGE Publications India Pvt. Ltd.
M-32 Market
Greater Kailash I
New Delhi 110 048 India

Printed in the United States of America

Library of Congress Cataloging-in-Publication Data

Main entry under title:

The survey kit.
    p. cm.
   Includes bibliographical references.
   Contents: v. 1. The survey handbook / Arlene Fink — v. 2. How to ask survey questions / Arlene Fink — v. 3. How to conduct self-administered and mail surveys / Linda B. Bourque, Eve P. Fielder — v. 4. How to conduct interviews by telephone and in person / James H. Frey, Sabine Mertens Oishi — v. 5. How to design surveys / Arlene Fink — v. 6. How to sample in surveys / Arlene Fink — v. 7. How to measure survey reliability and validity / Mark S. Litwin — v. 8. How to analyze survey data / Arlene Fink — v. 9. How to report on surveys / Arlene Fink.
   ISBN 0-8039-7388-8 (pbk. : The survey kit : alk. paper)
   1. Social surveys. 2. Health surveys. I. Fink, Arlene.
HN29.S724   1995
300′.723—dc20   95-12712

This book is printed on acid-free paper.

99 10 9 8 7 6 5

Sage Production Editor: Diane S. Foster
Sage Copy Editor: Joyce Kuhn
Sage Typesetter: Janelle LeMaster

Contents

How to Analyze Survey Data:
Learning Objectives

Surveys produce observations in the form of narrations or numbers. Narrations are responses stated in the survey participant's own words, which are then counted, compared, and interpreted, often using methods borrowed from communications theory and anthropology.

Numbers, or numerical data, are obtained when, for example, survey respondents may be asked to rate items on ordered, or ranked, scales, say, with 1 representing a very positive feeling and 5 representing a very negative one; in other surveys, participants may be asked to tell their age, height, or number of trips they have taken or books they have read. Survey data that take numerical form are analyzed using statistics, the mathematics of collecting, organizing, and interpreting numerical information.

The aim of this book is to teach you to become better users and consumers of statistics when applied in the analysis of survey data. It hopes to teach the basic vocabulary of statistics and the principles and logic behind the selection and interpretation of commonly used methods to analyze survey data. What the book does *not* do is teach you to be a survey statistician. For that, formal study is recommended, and, when appropriate, statistical consultation. If this book achieves its objectives, you will not only be able to tell the consultant exactly what you need but be able to interpret the data presented to you.

The specific objectives are to enable you to:

■ Learn the use of analytic terms, such as the following:

- Distribution
- Critical value
- Skew
- Transformation
- Measures of central tendency
- Dispersion
- Variation
- Statistical significance
- Practical significance
- p value
- Alpha
- Beta
- Linear
- Curvilinear
- Scatterplot
- Null hypothesis

■ List the steps to follow in selecting an appropriate analytic method

■ Distinguish between nominal, ordinal, and numerical scales and data so as to:

- Identify independent and dependent variables
- Distinguish between the appropriate uses of the mean, median, and mode
- Distinguish between the appropriate uses of the range, standard deviation, percentile rank, and interquartile range
- Understand the logic in and uses of correlations and regression
- Learn the steps in conducting and interpreting hypothesis tests
- Compare and contrast hypothesis testing and the use of confidence intervals
- Understand the logic in and uses of the chi-square distribution and test
- Understand the logic in and uses of the t test
- Understand the logic in and uses of analysis of variance
- Read and interpret computer output

1 What Statistics Do for Surveys

Statistics is the mathematics of organizing and interpreting numerical information. The results of statistical analyses are descriptions, relationships, comparisons, and predictions, as expressed in Example 1.1.

AUTHOR'S NOTE: The names of all corporations and survey instruments used in examples throughout this book are fictitious.

EXAMPLE 1.1
Statistical Analysis and Survey Data

A survey is given to 160 people to find out about the number and types of books they read. The survey is analyzed statistically to do the following:

- Describe the backgrounds of the respondents
- Describe the responses to each of the questions
- Determine if a connection exists between the number of books read and travel during the past year
- Compare the number of books read by men with the number read by women
- Find out if gender, education, or income predicts how frequently the respondents read books

Illustrative results are these:

1. *Describe respondents' background.* Of the survey's 160 respondents, 77 (48.1%) were men, with 72 (48%) earning more than $50,000 per year and having at least 2 years of college. Of the 150 respondents answering the question, 32 (21.3%) stated that they always or nearly always read for pleasure.

2. *Describe responses.* Respondents were asked how many books they read in a year and if they preferred fiction or nonfiction. On average, college graduates read 10 or more books, with a range of 2 to 50. The typical college graduate prefers nonfiction to fiction.

3. *Relationship between travel and number of books read.* Respondents were asked how often they traveled in the past year. Frequency of travel was compared to number of books read. Respondents who traveled at least twice in the past year read five or more books.

4. *Comparisons.* The percentage of men and women who read five or more books each year was compared, and no differences were found. On average, women's reading attitude scores were statistically significantly higher and more positive than men's, but older men's scores were significantly higher than older women's.

5. *Predicting frequency.* Education and income were found to be the best predictors of frequency of reading. That is, respondents with the most education and income read the most (one or more books each week).

In the first example, the findings are tallied and reported as percentages. A **tally** or **frequency count** is a computation of how many people fit into a category (men or women, under and over 70 years of age, read five or more books last year or did not). Tallies and frequencies take the form of numbers and percentages.

In the second example, the findings are presented as averages ("on average," "the typical" reader). When you are interested in the center (e.g., the average) of a distribution of findings, you are concerned with **measures of central tendency. Measures of dispersion** or spread, like the range, are often given along with measures of central tendency.

In the third example, the survey reports on the relationships between traveling and number of books read. One way of estimating the relationship between two characteristics is through **correlation.**

In the fourth example, comparisons are made between men and women. The term **statistical significance** is used to show that the differences between them are statistically meaningful and not due to chance.

In the fifth example, survey data are used to "predict" frequent reading. In simpler terms, predicting means answering a question like "Of all the characteristics on which I have survey data (e.g., income, education, type of books read, travel and leisure preferences), which one or ones are linked to frequent reading? For instance, does income make a difference? Education? Income and education?"

What methods should you use to describe, summarize, compare and predict? Before answering that question, you must answer at least four others: Do the survey data come from nominal, ordinal, or numerical scales or measures? How many independent and dependent variables are there? What statistical methods are potentially appropriate? Do the survey data fit the requirements of the methods?

Measurement Scales:
Nominal, Ordinal, and Numerical

A characteristic may be surveyed and measured using nominal, ordinal, and numerical scales. The resulting data are termed nominal, ordinal, or numerical.

NOMINAL SCALES

Nominal scales have no numerical value and produce data that fit into categories such as country of birth or gender. Nominal scales (and the data they yield) are sometimes called categorical scales or categorical data. Two survey questions resulting in nominal or categorical data are presented in Example 1.2.

EXAMPLE 1.2
Survey Questions That Use
Nominal Scales and Produce Nominal Data

1. What is the employee's gender? *Circle one*

Male	1
Female	2

2. Describe the type of lung cancer. *Circle one*

Small cell	1
Large cell	2
Oat cell	3
Squamous cell	4

Both questions categorize the responses. The answer is the "name" of the category into which the data fit. The numbers are arbitrary and have no inherent value. In Question 1, female could be labeled 1 and male 2. The numbers are merely codes.

When nominal data take on one of two values as in the first question (e.g., male or female), they are termed **dichotomous**. Nominal data are also called **categorical**.

ORDINAL SCALES

If an inherent order exists among categories, the data are said to have been obtained from an ordinal scale, as illustrated in Example 1.3.

EXAMPLE 1.3
Survey Questions That Use Ordinal Scales

1. How much education have you completed? *Circle one*

Never finished high school	1
High school graduate but no college	2
Some college	3
College graduate	4

2. Stage of tumor. *Circle one*

Duke's A	1
Duke's B	2
Duke's C	3
Duke's D	4

3. How often during the past month did you find yourself having difficulty trying to calm down? *Circle one*

Always	5
Very often	4
Fairly often	3
Sometimes	2
Almost never	1

Ordinal scales typically are seen in questions that call for ratings of quality (e.g., excellent, very good, good, fair, poor, very poor) and agreement (e.g., strongly agree, agree, disagree, strongly disagree).

NUMERICAL (INTERVAL AND RATIO) SCALES

When differences between numbers have a meaning on a numerical scale, they are called numerical. Age is a numerical variable, and so is weight and length of survival after diagnosis of a serious disease. Numerical data lend themselves to precision, so you can obtain data on age to the nearest second, for example.

You may hear the terms interval and ratio scales. Interval scales have an arbitrary zero point like the Fahrenheit and Celsius temperature scales. The difference, or distance, between 40° and 50° Celsius is the same as the difference between 70° and 80°. But 40° is not twice as hot as 20°, and 0° does not mean no heat at all. Ratio scales, however, have a true zero point, as in the absolute zero value of the Kelvin scale. Practically speaking, ratio scales are extremely rare, and statistically, interval and ratio scales are treated the same; hence the term numerical is a more apt (and neutral) phrase.

Numerical data can be **continuous**—height, weight, age—or discrete—numbers of visits to this clinic, numbers of previous pregnancies. Means and standard deviations are used to summarize the values of numerical measures.

The three measurement scales and their data types are contrasted in the following table.

Measurement Scale and Type of Data	Examples	Comments
Nominal	Type of disease: small-cell, large-cell, oat-cell, and squamous-cell cancer; grade in school: 9th, 10th, 11th, 12th; ethnicity; gender	Observations belong to categories. Observations have no inherent order of importance. Observations sometimes are called categorical.
Ordinal	Ratings of health status (excellent, very good, good, fair, poor) and of agreement (strongly agree, agree, disagree, strongly disagree); rankings (the top 10 movies)	Order exists among the categories—that is, one observation is of greater value than the other or more important.
Numerical	Continuous numerical scales: scores on an achievement test or attitude inventory; age; height; length of survival Discrete numerical scales: number of visits to a physician; number of falls; number of days absent from work or class	Differences between numbers have meaning on a numerical scale (e.g., higher scores mean better achievement than lower scores, and a difference between 12 and 13 has the same meaning as a difference between 99 and 100). Some statisticians distinguish between interval scales (arbitrary 0 point, as in the Fahrenheit scale) and ratio scales (absolute 0, as in the Kelvin scale); these measures are usually treated the same statistically, so they are combined here as numerical.

Independent and Dependent Variables

A **variable** is a characteristic that is measurable. Weight is a variable, and all persons weighing 55 kilograms have the same numerical weight. Satisfaction with a product is also a variable. In this case, however, the numerical scale has to be devised and rules must be created for its interpretation. For example, in Survey A, product satisfaction is measured on a scale from 1 to 100, with 100 representing perfect satisfaction. Survey B, however, measures satisfaction by counting the number of repeat customers. The rule is that at least 15% of all customers must reorder within a year for a demonstration of satisfaction.

Your choice of method for analyzing survey data is always dependent on the type of data available to you (nominal, ordinal, and numerical) and on the number of variables that is involved. Some survey variables are termed **independent,** and some are termed **dependent.**

Independent variables are also called "explanatory" or "predictor" variables because they are used to explain or predict a response, outcome, or result—the dependent variable. The independent and dependent variables can be identified by studying the objectives and target of the survey, as illustrated in Example 1.4.

EXAMPLE 1.4
Targets and Independent Variables

Objective 1: To describe the quality of life of men over 65 years of age with different health characteristics (e.g., whether or not they have hypertension or diabetes) and social backgrounds (e.g., whether they live alone or live with someone; if they are employed or unemployed). The men in the survey had surgery for prostate cancer within the past 2 years.

Target: Men over 65 years of age with differing health characteristics and social backgrounds who have had surgery for prostate cancer within the past 2 years

Independent variables: Age (over 65 years of age), health characteristics (presence or absence of hypertension or diabetes), and social background (living alone or not and employment status)

Dependent variable: Quality of life

Objective 2: To compare elementary school children in different grades in two ways: (a) opinions on the school's new dress code and (b) attitude toward school

Target: Boys and girls in Grades 3 through 6 in five elementary schools

Independent variables: Gender, grade level, and school

Dependent variables: Opinion of new dress code and attitude toward school

Objective 1 has three independent variables and one dependent variable; Objective 2 has three independent and two dependent variables. A next step in the analytic process is to determine whether the survey's data for these variables are nominal, ordinal, or numerical. Look at Example 1.5.

EXAMPLE 1.5
Are Data Nominal, Ordinal, or Numerical?

Survey 1: Men With Prostate Cancer

Independent Variables
- Age (over 65 years of age)
- Health characteristics (presence or absence of hypertension or diabetes)
- Social background (whether living alone or not and employment status)

Characteristics of Survey Questions
- To get age, ask for exact birth date.
- To find out about health characteristics, ask "Do you have any of the following medical conditions? Answer yes or no for each."
- To find out about social background, ask respondents to answer yes or no regarding whether or not they live alone and are presently employed full-time, part-time, or not employed at all.

Type of Data
- Age: Numerical (birth date)
- Health characteristics: Nominal (presence or absence of medical conditions)

- Social background: Nominal (live alone or do not; employed or not)

Dependent Variable
- Quality of life

Characteristics of Survey Questions
- Ask questions that call for ratings of various aspects of quality of life. For example, ask respondents to describe how frequently they feel restless, down in the dumps, rattled, moody, and so on.
- Use categories for the responses, such as all of the time, most of the time, a good bit of the time, some of the time, a little of the time, none of the time.

Type of Data
- Quality of life: Ordinal (May be numerical if statistical evidence exists that higher scores are statistically and practically different from lower scores)

Survey 2: Children, Dress Code, and Attitude Toward School

Independent Variables
- Gender
- Grade level
- Schools

Characteristics of Survey Questions
- To get gender, ask if male or female.
- Ask participants to write in grade level and name of school.

Type of Data
- Gender: Nominal
- Grade level: Nominal
- Name of School: Nominal

Dependent Variables
- Opinion of new dress code
- Attitude toward school

Characteristics of Survey Questions
- To get opinions on new dress code, ask for ratings of like and dislike (e.g., from like a lot to dislike a lot).
- To learn about attitudes, use the Attitude Toward School Rating Scale.

Type of Data
- Opinions of dress code: Ordinal
- Attitudes: Ordinal

When choosing an appropriate analysis method, you begin by deciding on the purpose of the analysis, and then you determine the number of independent and dependent variables and whether you have nominal, ordinal, or numerical data. When these activities are completed, you can choose an analysis method. Example 1.6 shows how this works in two hypothetical cases. (In the example, two statistical methods are mentioned. Their uses are discussed later.)

EXAMPLE 1.6
Choosing an Analysis Method

Survey Objective: To compare scores on the Quality of Life Inventory achieved by men who are employed full-time, part-time, or unemployed and who had surgery for prostate cancer 2 years ago.

Number of Independent Variables: One (employment status)
Type of data: Nominal (employed full-time, employed part-time, unemployed)

Number of Dependent Variables: One (quality of life)
Type of data: Numerical (scores)
Name of Possible Method of Analysis: One-way analysis of variance

Survey Objective: To compare boys and girls with differing scores on the Attitude Toward School Questionnaire in terms of whether they do or do not support the school's new dress code

Number of Independent Variables: One (gender)
Type of data: Nominal (boys, girls)

Number of Dependent Variables: One (support dress code)
Type of data: Nominal (support or do not support)
Possible Method of Analysis: Logistic regression

In Example 1.6, both choices of analytic method are labeled "possible." The appropriateness of the choice of a statistical method depends upon the extent to which you meet the method's *assumptions* about the characteristics and quality of the data. In the preceding examples, too little information is given to help you decide on whether the assumptions are met.

The aim of the discussion that follows is to guide you in understanding the logic behind the choice of an analytic method. The discussion gives examples of the formulas and use of some of the most commonly accepted statistical procedures and describes their assumptions. The idea is not to turn you into a survey statistician but to guide you in obtaining the information you need to choose the correct analysis. When implementing the analysis, the calculations are only meaningful if they are the ones you need and if the data are available and clean.

The following checklist should be used *before* you choose an analysis method.

Checklist for Choosing a Method to Analyze Survey Data

✓ **Count the number of independent variables.**

✓ **Determine if the data on the independent variables are nominal, ordinal, or numerical.**

✓ **Count the number of dependent variables.**

✓ **Determine if the data on the dependent variables are nominal, ordinal, or numerical.**

✓ **Choose potential data-analytic methods.**

✓ **Screen the survey's objectives (description, relationship, prediction, comparison) against the analysis method's assumptions and outcomes.**

Descriptive Statistics and Measures of Central Tendency: Numerical and Ordinal Data

Descriptive statistics describe data in terms of measures of central tendency. These are measures or statistics that describe the location of the center of a distribution. A **distribution** consists of values (e.g., scores and other numerical values, such as number of years in office, age in years as of today) of a variable or characteristic (e.g., attitudes, knowledge, behavior, health status, and demographics, such as age, income, etc.) and the frequency of their occurrence. For example, in a survey that asks if the respondent is under 25 years of age or 25 years and older, the distribution consists of the ages (with the values: under 25 years and 25 years and older) and the frequency (the number of respondents in each of the two age categories). In a survey that produces scores on a scale from 1 to 10, the distribution of scores consists of the numbers of people who achieve a score of 1, 2, and so on to a score of 10.

Measures of dispersion are descriptive statistics that depict the spread of numerical data. For example, in a survey that produces scores on a scale from 1 to 10, you calculate measures of dispersion to answer questions like "Are most of the scores clustered around a single score, say 5?" and "What is the highest score? The lowest?"

Measures of central tendency are the mean, median, and mode. Measures of dispersion or spread are the range, standard deviation, and percentiles.

MEAN

The **mean** is the arithmetic average of observations. It is symbolized as $\overline{X}$. You calculate the mean by totaling observations (scores or responses) and dividing by the number of observations.

The formula is $\Sigma X/n$. Σ is the Greek letter sigma, and it means to add or sum. X is each individual observation, and n is the total number of observations.

Example 1.7 shows the calculation of the mean.

EXAMPLE 1.7
Calculating the Mean

Students who took the 20-point Attitude Toward Spelling Survey received these 15 scores:

$$-6, -3, -3, 0, 2, 2, 2, 3, 3, 3, 3, 4, 4, 5, 6.$$

The mean $(\Sigma X/n)$ of the scores is

$$(-6) + (-3) + (-3) + (0) + (2) + (2) + (2) + (3) + (3) +$$
$$(3) + (3) + (4) + (4) + (5) + (6) = 25/15 = 1.67.$$

Suppose the 15th student obtained a score of 20 (rather than 6). The mean would be 39/15, or 2.6. The mean is sensitive to extreme values in a set of observations.

You can only use the mean when the numbers you have can be added or when characteristics are measured on a numerical scale like those used to describe height, weight, and scores on a test.

MEDIAN

The median is the middle observation. Half of the observations are smaller and half are larger. No abbreviation or symbol is commonly used for the median. Because it falls in the middle, the median is sometimes considered the "typical" observation.

You determine the median by doing the following:

1. Arrange the observations (scores, responses) from lowest to highest (or vice versa).
2. Count to the middle value. The median is the middle value for an odd number of observations and is the mean of the two middle values for an even number of observations.

Consider this odd number of scores:

$$3, 6, 6, 7, 9, 13, 17.$$

The median is 7 because half of the scores (3, 6, 6) are below 7 and half (9, 13, 17) are above.

Take this even number of scores:

$$-2, 0, 6, 7, 9, 9.$$

The two middle scores are 6 and 7. If you add 6 + 7 and divide by 2, you get the median, 6.5.

EXERCISES

1. Calculate the median for the following:

   2, 4, 5, 8, 9, 11.

2. Calculate the median for the following:

   3, 9, 7, −2, 6, 7.

■ ANSWERS ■

1. Median is 6.5.
2. Rearrange so that you have 9, 7, 7, 6, 3, −2 for a median of 6.5.

The median is not as sensitive as the mean to extreme values. So, if you have a few "outliers" in the distribution, you will probably want to use the median.

MODE

The mode of a distribution is the value of the observations that occurs most frequently. It is commonly used when you want to show the most "popular" value.

Distribution A		Distribution B	
Score	Frequency	Score	Frequency
34	2	34	0
33	6	33	1
32	8	32	7
31	11	31	21
30	15	30	4
29	18	29	3
28	10	28	7
27	12	27	10
26	8	26	14
25	3	25	23
24	1	24	11
23	0	23	5

Distribution A has a single mode of 29, with 18 responses. This distribution is **unimodal.** Distribution B has two modes, at 25 and 31, so the distribution is **bimodal.**

Distributions: Skewed and Symmetric

When you have a distribution that has a few outlying observations in one direction—a few small values or a few large ones
—it is termed **skewed.** A **symmetric** distribution is one in
which the distribution has the same shape on both sides of the
mean.

Figure 1–1 shows that if the mean and median are equal, the
distribution of observations is symmetric (A). If the mean is
smaller than the median, the distribution is skewed to the left
(B). If the mean is larger than the median, the distribution is
skewed to the right (C).

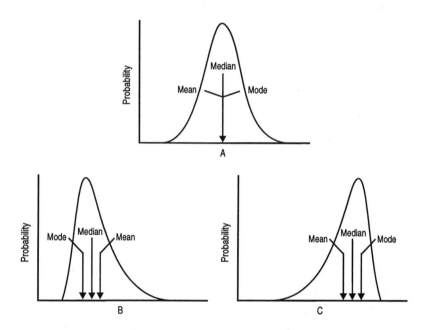

Figure 1–1. Distributions: Skewed and Symmetric
SOURCE: *Statistical First Aid* (p. 32), by R. Hirsch and R. K. Riegelman,
1992, Cambridge, MA: Blackwell Scientific. Copyright 1992 by Blackwell
Scientific Publications, Inc. Used with permission.

Checklist for Using the
Mean, Median, and Mode

✓ Use the *mean* when:

- The distribution is approximately symmetric.
- You are interested in numerical values.

✓ Use the *median* when:

- You are concerned with the typical score.
- The distribution is skewed.
- You have ordinal data.

✓ Use the *mode* when:

- The distribution has two or more peaks.
- You want the prevailing view, characteristic, or quality.

Measures of Spread

Suppose you ask a group of people to rate the quality of food at a particular restaurant. You find that the average rating is 3.5 on a scale of 1 (*poor*) to 5 (*excellent*). How close in agreement are the people? Do their ratings cluster around 3 (the middle point), or are the ratings **spread**, with some people assigning ratings of 1 and the remainder 5?

The extent of spread, or the **dispersion** or **variation,** of the observations is described by the range, standard deviation, percentile, and interquartile range.

RANGE

The **range** is the difference between the largest observation and the smallest. Sometimes, the range is expressed by highest and lowest values rather than just the difference between them. Example 1.8 demonstrates how the range is used.

EXAMPLE 1.8
Using the Range

These are the scores achieved by 10 people on the 20-item Survey of Compassionate Behavior:

4, 7, 9, 11, 11, 12, 14, 16, 17, 18.

The range is 14 points. The scores ranged from 4 to 18.

STANDARD DEVIATION

The **standard deviation** is a measure of the spread of data about their mean and an essential part of many statistical tests. Although it is highly unlikely that you will compute a standard deviation by hand, it is useful to see how the standard deviation functions.

The standard deviation (SD) depends on calculating the average distance that the average score is from the mean. The definitional formula is

$$SD = \sqrt{\Sigma (X - \overline{X})^2/(n - 1)}$$

Suppose you had the following 10 scores on the Survey of Compassionate Behavior:

7, 10, 8, 5, 4, 8, 4, 9, 7, 8.

Here is how to calculate the standard deviation.

- Compute the mean:

  1. $\overline{X} = (7 + 10 + 8 + 5 + 4 + 8 + 4 + 9 + 7 + 8)/10 = 7$.
  2. Subtract the mean $(\overline{X})$ from each score (X), or $X - \overline{X}$.
  3. Square each remainder from Step 2, or $(X - \overline{X})^2$.

Score	Step 2 $(X - \overline{X})$	Step 3 $(X - \overline{X})^2$
7	$(7 - 7) = 0$	0
10	$(10 - 7) = 3$	9
8	$(8 - 7) = 1$	1
5	$(5 - 7) = -2$	4
4	$(4 - 7) = -3$	9
8	$(8 - 7) = 1$	1
4	$(4 - 7) = -3$	9
9	$(9 - 7) = 2$	4
7	$(7 - 7) = 0$	0
8	$(8 - 7) = 1$	1

  4. Sum (Σ) all the squares from Step 3, or $\Sigma(X - \overline{X})^2$:

$$\Sigma(X - \overline{X})^2 = 0 + 9 + 1 + 4 + 9 + 1 + 9 + 4 + 0 + 1 = 38.$$

  5. Divide the number in Step 4 by $n - 1$.

$$38/n - 1 = 38/9 = 4.22.$$

A digression: n is the number of scores; $n - 1$ is used because it produces a more accurate estimate of the true population's standard deviation and has other desirable mathematical properties. The quantity $n - 1$ is called the **degrees of freedom,** a concept that appears in other statistical formulas and tables. (The term degrees of freedom sounds intuitively meaningful but is in fact a complex statistical concept that is discussed in advanced texts and is well beyond the scope of this book.)

6. Take the square root of the result of Step 5.

$$\sqrt{4.22} = 2.05.$$

The standard deviation squared is called the **variance.** In the above example, the variance is 4.22. This statistic is not used as often as the standard deviation, which has two characteristics that should be kept in mind:

- Regardless of how the survey observations are distributed, at least 75% of them will always fall between the mean plus 2 standard deviations $(\overline{X} + 2SD)$ and the mean minus 2 standard deviations $(\overline{X} - 2SD)$. Suppose the mean of 32 scores is 12 and the standard deviation is 1.2. At least 75% of the 32 scores, or 24 scores, will be between $12 + 2(1.2)$ and $12 - 2(1.2)$, or between 14.4 and 9.6.
- Check to see if the distribution of the scores is symmetric (bell-shaped or normal), as shown in Figure 1-2. If so, then the following rules apply:

  About 68% of all observations fall between the mean and 1 standard deviation.

  About 95% of all observations fall between the mean and 2 standard deviations.

  About 99% of all observations fall between the mean and 3 standard deviations.

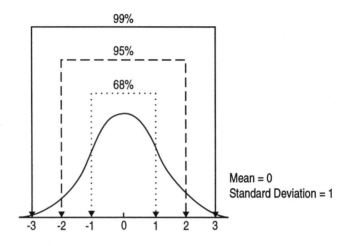

Figure 1–2. Normal Distribution

PERCENTILE

A **percentile** is a number that indicates the percentage of a distribution that is equal to or below that number. To say that a person scored in the 95th percentile means that 95% of others scored the same or below that person. Percentiles are often used to compare an individual value with a set of standards. Obtaining a reading score in the 30th percentile means that, compared to a standard or norm such as statewide scores, 30% have the same or lower scores and 70% have the same or higher scores. The median is the 50th percentile: Half of the distribution is at or above, and half is at or below.

INTERQUARTILE RANGE

A measure of variation that makes use of percentiles is the **interquartile range,** which is the difference between the 25th and the 75th percentile. The interquartile range contains 50%

of the observations. For example, suppose students at the 25th percentile have an average score of 30.2, and those at the 75th have a score of 90.1. The central 50% of the scores, or the interquartile range, is the difference between 90.1 (the 75th percentile) and 30.2 (the 25th). Another way to put it is that 50% of the students achieved scores between 30.2 and 90.1.

Guidelines for Selecting Measures of Dispersion

- *Range.* Numerical (e.g., scores from 1 to 100). The range describes the highest and lowest scores.
- *Standard deviation.* Numerical. Standard deviations describe the spread of means.
- *Percentile.* Ordinal (e.g., ratings on a scale from 1 = *very bad* to 5 = *very good*) or numerical (e.g., scores). The median is the 50th percentile.
- *Interquartile range.* Ordinal or numerical. The interquartile range is the central 50% of a set of observations or the difference between the 75th and the 25th percentile.

Descriptive Statistics and Nominal Data

Survey characteristics that are measured on a nominal scale do not have numerical values, but you can count them and describe how frequently they occur. Typical survey questions producing nominal data are the following:

Did you read these books?

Jane Eyre	Yes	No
Schindler's List	Yes	No

Which best describes your current living status?
    Circle one only.

Living alone	Yes	No
Living with a friend, not related	Yes	No
Living with a relative	Yes	No
Living in a communal arrangement	Yes	No
Other (specify _____)	Yes	No

For each question and its component parts, the choices are yes or no: Yes, I read *Jane Eyre*, or no, I did not; yes, I live alone, or no, I do not; and so on. Nominal survey data are analyzed by using descriptive statistics such as proportion, percentage, ratio, and rate.

PROPORTION AND PERCENTAGE

A **proportion** is the number of observations or responses with a given characteristic divided by the total number of observations. Look at the following table.

Table 1–1
Perceptions of an Experimental and Control Group

Outcome	Experimental Group	Control Group
Felt better	65	73
Felt worse	4	10
Total	69	83

A proportion is a *part* divided by a *whole*. Using the data in Table 1–1, the proportion who felt better in the experimental group is 65 divided by the total number of responses in the experimental group (better and worse), which is 69, or 65/69, or .9420. In the control group, the proportion who felt better is 73/83, or .8795.

A **percentage** is a proportion multiplied by 100%, so the percentage of people who felt better in the experimental group is .9420 × 100%, or 94.2%, while the percentage who felt better in the control is .8795 × 100%, or 87.9% rounded off to 88%.

The proportion is a special case of the mean in which the observations with a given characteristic, say, people who felt better, are assigned the value 1, and the observations without the characteristic, say, people who felt worse, are assigned the value 0. The sum X in the numerator of the formula for the mean is the sum of the 0s and 1s and the denominator is still n (the number of observations). So, the proportion of people (Table 1–1) who felt better is (65 × 1) + (4 × 0)/69, or .9420.

RATIO AND RATE

A **ratio** is a *part* divided by another *part*. It is the number of observations in a given group with a certain characteristic (e.g., feeling better) divided by the number of observations without the given characteristic (e.g., feeling worse). In Table 1–1, the ratio of feeling better to feeling worse in the experimental group is 65/4, or 16.25. The ratio of feeling better to feeling worse in the control is 73/10, or 7.3.

The **rate** is similar to the proportion except that a multiplier or **base**—1,000, 10,000, 100,000—is used. Rates are always computed over time, say, a year. Using the data in Table 1–1, suppose the experimental group participated in a study for a year, and the base was chosen to be 1,000. The rate of feeling better per 1,000 persons per year is then 65/69 × 1,000, or about 942 persons for each 1,000 per year.

2 Relationships or Correlation

Numerical Data

A relationship is a consistent association between or among variables. Suppose four surveys ask four questions:

1. Are the readers of this magazine also financially well off?
2. Do children who visit the school nurse most often have low self-concepts?
3. Do two observers agree on what they see?
4. Do people who do well in the program read well?

These questions are about relationships. For Question 1, the relationship of interest is between readers and financial well-being; for Question 2, between frequency of visits to the school nurse and self-concept; for Question 3, between what Observers 1 and 2 see; and for Question 4, between success in the program and high reading ability.

When you are concerned with the relationship between two variables, you are ready for correlation analysis. When the two variables are expressed numerically, you use a **correlation coefficient,** sometimes called a Pearson product-moment coefficient (after the statistician who discovered it). The correlation coefficient has a range of +1 to –1.

Consider two variables, X and Y. X is the independent variable, and Y is the dependent variable. A perfect correlation of +1 means that the value of Y increases by the same amount for each unit of increase in the value of X. A correlation of –1 indicates a perfect inverse relationship, in which the value of the dependent variable decreases by the same amount for each unit increase in the value of the independent variable. A correlation coefficient of zero indicates that no relationship exists between the dependent and independent variables. In other words, no consistent (that is, in one direction only) change in the value of the dependent variable occurs for each unit change in the value of the independent variable.

What do correlation coefficients mean? If you examine correlations graphically, you can see that the stronger the correlation (that is, the closer to +1 or to –1), the more it resembles a straight line. This is called a **linear** relationship.

Correlations are described graphically as a **scatterplot** in which the numerical values of the two variables are expressed as points. Figure 2–1a shows a perfect negative correlation (–1) between two variables; Figure 2–1b, a perfect positive correlation (+1); and Figure 2–1c, no correlation at all. As you can see, the correlations of +1 and –1 look like a line. When a correlation is near zero, the shape of the pattern of observations is spread throughout and is somewhat circular. A correlation of .50 tends to be more oval.

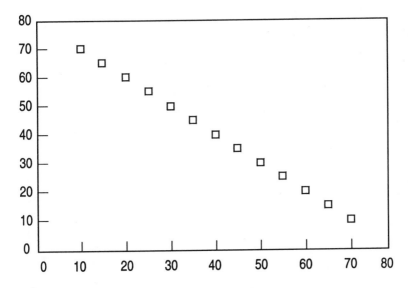

Figure 2–1a. Perfect Negative Correlation

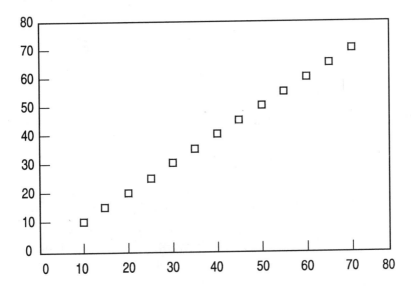

Figure 2–1b. Perfect Positive Correlation

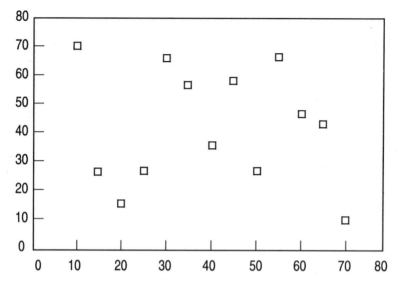

Figure 2–1c.   Correlation of Zero

Calculating the Correlation Coefficient

The correlation coefficient is symbolized as r and is usually reported in two decimal places, and the formula for calculating r is

$$r = \frac{\Sigma(X - \overline{X})\,(Y - \overline{Y})}{\sqrt{\Sigma(X - \overline{X})^2}\ \sqrt{\Sigma(Y - \overline{Y})^2}}.$$

The data used in the following calculation come from a survey to determine if a relationship exists between years of education and number of books read in the past year. X is the independent variable (years of education). Y is the dependent variable (number of books read in the past year). Ten people participated in the survey.

Respondent	X	Y	$X-\bar{X}$ ($\bar{X}=9.5$)	$Y-\bar{Y}$ ($\bar{Y}=11.8$)	$(X-\bar{X})(Y-\bar{Y})$	$(X-\bar{X})^2$	$(Y-\bar{Y})^2$
1	10	12	.5	.2	.1	.2	.04
2	12	14	2.5	2.2	5.5	6.2	4.8
3	5	7	−4.5	−4.8	21.6	20.2	23.0
4	7	9	−2.5	−2.8	7.0	6.2	7.8
5	7	10	−2.5	−1.8	4.5	6.2	3.2
6	12	15	2.5	3.2	8.0	6.2	10.2
7	10	13	.5	1.2	.6	.2	1.4
8	6	8	−3.5	−3.8	13.3	12.2	14.4
9	10	12	.5	.2	.1	.2	.04
10	16	18	6.5	6.2	40.3	42.3	38.4
Sum	95	118			101	100.1	103.3

1. Using the table above to get each Σ in the formula, you see that

$$\Sigma(X - \bar{X})(Y - \bar{Y}) = 101;$$
$$S(X - \bar{X})^2(Y - \bar{Y})^2 = 101.1 \times 103.$$

2. Filling in the formula, you get the following:
   a. $101/\sqrt{100.1}\ \sqrt{103.3}$
      $\sqrt{100.1} = 10.0$ (rounded)
      $\sqrt{100.3} = 10.2$ (rounded)
   b. $101/10 \times 10.2$
      $10 \times 10.2 = 102$
   c. $101/102 = .99$

The correlation coefficient is .99, suggesting a nearly perfect relationship between years of education and number of books read in the past year.

A correlation coefficient measures only a straight-line, or **linear,** relationship. If the distribution of data for either the independent or the dependent variable is skewed or contains outlying values, then you have a **curvilinear** relationship. In this case, a **transformation** of the data is warranted so that you can use conventional statistical methods. (Otherwise, you cannot.) When you transform data, you change the scale of measurement. How do you know if the relationship is curvilinear? You should always plot the relationship. Use the computer to do this unless you have a relatively small sample and the time to plot the relationship by hand on graph paper.

Size of the Correlation

How Large Should a Correlation Be?
A Conservative Rule of Thumb

0 to +.25 (or −.25) = Little or no relationship

+.26 to +.50 (or −.26 to −.50) = Fair degree of relationship

+.51 to +.75 = (or −.51 to −.75) = Moderate to good relationship

Over +.75 (or −.75) = Very good to excellent relationship

For some social science disciplines, correlations of .26 to .50 are considered quite high, especially if they occur in multiple regression models where one variable is estimated by the use of more than one other variable.

The adequacy of the correlation is largely situational. For example, if the correlation between scores on your new and supposedly efficient attitude inventory and the older, supposedly more cumbersome one is .75, you might feel just fine until you find out that the correlation between someone else's inventory and the older one is .90.

Other than for values of +1, 0, and –1, however, correlation coefficients are not easy to interpret. We know, for example, that two variables with a correlation of .50 have a direct but imperfect relationship. Can we say that a correlation of .50 is half that of 1? Actually, to answer this question, you must make use of another statistic: **the coefficient of determination,** or r^2.

The r^2 tells the proportion of variation in the dependent variable that is associated with variation or changes in the independent variable. For a correlation coefficient of .50, the coefficient of determination is $.50^2$, or .25. This means that 25% of the variation in one measure (e.g., number of books read) may be predicted by knowing the value of the other (e.g., years of education)—or the other way around. A correlation of .50 describes an association that is one quarter as strong as a correlation of 1. In the example above (years of education and number of books read) where the correlation coefficient is .99, the coefficient of determination is .99 × .99, or 98%. In this case, 98% of the variation in number of books read can be predicted by knowing years of education—or the other way around.

WARNING

 Use correlations to estimate the relationship between two characteristics. Do NOT use them to establish cause and effect, or **causation**. A correlation analysis can show that years of education and numbers of books read are strongly related, but it cannot confirm that people read many books because they have many years of education. For one thing, a preference for reading may be the cause of many years of education, or years of education and number of books may be "caused" by a third factor—for example, a relatively high income.

Ordinal Data and Correlation

The Spearman (the statistician's name) rank correlation, sometimes called Spearman's rho, is often used to describe the relationship between two ordinal or one ordinal and one numerical characteristic, as in Example 2.1.

EXAMPLE 2.1
Using Spearman's Rho

To describe relationships between two ordinal characteristics

Does a relationship exist between ratings of satisfaction and of preferences for leisure time activities?

Does a relationship exist between level of education and ratings of satisfaction?

To describe relationships between one ordinal and one numerical characteristic

Does a relationship exist between level of education and quantity of sports equipment purchased in the past year?

Does a relationship exist between preference ratings and number of trips taken for pleasure?

Spearman's rho is also used with numerical data when the observations are skewed, with respondent outliers. In fact, if the median is the appropriate statistic to measure central tendency, then Spearman's rho is the correct correlation procedure.

The symbol for Spearman's rho is r_s. To calculate r_s, put the data in "rank" order (e.g., from highest to lowest score). Spearman's rho involves tedious computations and should be done by computer.

Spearman's rho ranges from +1 to –1, with + and –1 meaning perfect correlation between the ranks rather than the numerical values.

Regression

One of the major differences between correlation and regression is that correlation describes a relationship and regression predicts a value. Regression analysis is concerned with estimating the components of a mathematical model that reflects the relationship between the dependent and independent variables in the population. To make the estimate, you assume that the relationship between variables is linear and that a straight line can be used to summarize the data. Regression is often referred to as linear regression, or simple linear regression. There is, however, nothing simple about regression analysis. Although you should understand its uses and how to interpret the results, you probably need more information than is presented here to actually conduct the analysis or to debate with a statistician the virtues of the alternative regression methods.

A common method for fitting a line to the data or observations is called least squares. Suppose you interview a sample of teenaged mothers to determine the extent to which County A's outreach program was responsible for encouraging them to keep their recommended number of prenatal care appointments. The regression equation would look like this:

Predicted number of visits = a + b (outreach).

This equation can be illustrated graphically, as shown in Figure 2–2.

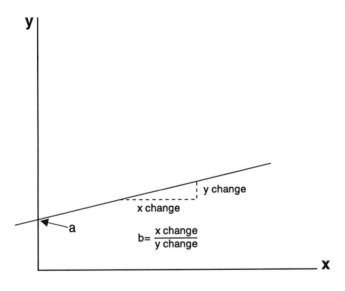

Figure 2–2. Graphic Interpretation of Regression Line

In the figure, you see a Y-axis (vertical) and an X-axis (horizontal). The line intercepts the Y-axis at *a* (called the **intercept**). The slope of the line measures the amount of change in Y for each unit change in X. If the slope is positive, Y increases as X increases; if the slope is negative, Y decreases as X increases. In the example above, in which your interest is the ability to relate prenatal care visits and the county's outreach teen program, *a* is the predicted number of visits without outreach. The slope, *b*, is the change in predicted number of visits for a unit of change in outreach. Stated another way, *b* is the amount of change in number of visits per outreach activity.

In regression, the slope in the population is symbolized by the Greek letter beta, or β_1, called the regression coefficient; β_0 denotes the intercept of the regression line. Also, the values of the Ys provided from the regression equation are predicted rather than actual values. Predicted values are distinguished from actual values by using the symbol $Y_{\prime}$. Because not all predictions are perfect, the regression model contains an error term, *e*. This is the amount the actual values of Y depart from the predicted values based on the regression line. The formula for the regression model is

$$Y_{\prime} = \beta_0 + \beta_1 X + e.$$

A Note on the Relationship
Between Two Nominal Characteristics

Surveys are usually interested in the significance of the relationship between two nominal variables rather than in just the relationship itself. You are more likely to be concerned with determining if the number of women answering yes to a particular question is statistically different from the number of men answering yes than you are in the extent of agreement between the number of women and men answering yes. Among the techniques for determining the significance of the differences between nominal variables are chi-square and Fisher's exact test. The chi-square distribution is described in Chapter 3. To use it appropriately, the normal distribution and hypothesis testing should be understood first.

The Normal Distribution

The normal distribution is a smooth, bell-shaped curve that is continuous and symmetric around the mean, which is symbolized by μ (Greek letter mu). The standard deviation is symbolized by σ (Greek lowercase letter sigma). The mean ±1 standard deviation contains approximately 68% of the area under the normal curve; the mean ±2 standard deviations contains approximately 95% of the area under the normal curve, and the mean ±3 standard deviations contains approximately 99% of the area under the normal curve.

A normally distributed random variable with a mean and standard deviation can be transformed to a **standard normal,** or **z distribution.** This distribution has a mean of 0 and a standard deviation of 1.

The **z transformation** expresses the deviation from the mean in standard deviation units. Any normal distribution can be transformed to the z distribution by using this formula:

$$z = X - \beta/\sigma.$$

But what is a normal distribution of survey data or observations, and how do you know if you have one? When you study the **population at large,** certain variables like height, weight, blood pressure, and so on are considered normally distributed, that is, with 99% of the observations falling within ±3 standard deviations of the mean. In actuality, perfectly normal distributions are as rare as perfectly normal people. This is true even for the distribution of height, weight, and blood pressure. Some distributions like these, however, are more normal than others.

Many computer programs will tell you graphically if a distribution is normal. If you prefer, you can plot the data yourself in the form of a histogram or box-and-whisker plot. A histogram uses area to describe the frequency distribution of numerical observations.

If a distribution is normal, then you can use statistical methods that assume normality, such as the *t* test. If not, you must transform the data to make them normal or use statistical methods that are not dependent on normal distributions.

Comparisons: Hypothesis Testing, *p* Values, and Confidence Levels

Surveys often compare two or more groups such as men and women, experimental and control participants, Team A and Team B, and students in the United States and students elsewhere. If differences exist, the magnitude is analyzed for significance. When comparing one nominal independent variable (e.g., experimental and control group) with respect to one numerical dependent variable (e.g., attitudes as measured by a score), a two-sample independent groups *t* test can be used. This statistical test, one of the most common, is illustrated in Example 2.2.

In the example, a survey is conducted after 2 years to find out if an experimental protocol affecting the management practices of a private company has improved the quality and efficiency of the cafeterias in selected schools. A survey is given to participating and nonparticipating schools, and the results are compared. The survey has 100 points; a 15-point difference is needed in favor of the private company for the experiment to be considered a success.

EXAMPLE 2.2
Comparing Two Groups: The *t* Test

Situation

The schools' cafeterias have always been run by employees of the school district. In recent years, the quality and efficiency of the cafeterias have diminished. An outside consulting group is called in to recommend ways to improve the management of the cafeterias. The consultants suggest that a private company, rather than the district, may have the answer. The district agrees. After a bidding process, a contract is awarded to the Great Food Company to manage several school cafeterias. After 2 years, students, teachers, administrators, and other school personnel are surveyed regarding their opinions of the quality of the food and the service and the efficiency of Great Food's operation.

Expectations

A statistically significant difference in opinions will be found favoring Great Food over the district. Opinions will be assessed using the results of a 100-point survey.

Analysis

A *t* test will be applied in comparing the two groups' opinions of quality and efficiency.

In Example 2.2, mention is made of **statistical significance.** This is a very important term. To be significant, differences must be attributable to a planned intervention (e.g., Great

Food's new management efforts) rather than to chance or historical occurrences (e.g., a change in expectations regarding the cafeteria that comes about because most students eat somewhere else).

Statistical significance is often interpreted to mean a result that happens by chance less than once in 20 times, with a *p* value less than or equal to .05. A *p* value is the probability of obtaining the results of a statistical test by chance. The null hypothesis states that no difference exists in the means (scores or other numerical values) obtained by two groups. Statistical significance occurs when the null hypothesis is rejected (suggesting that a difference does exist).

The following is a more detailed explanation of these terms and a guide for conducting a hypothesis test and determining statistical significance.

Guide to Hypothesis Testing, Statistical Significance, and *p* Values

1. *State the null hypothesis.* The null hypothesis (H_o) is a statement that no difference exists between the averages or means of two groups. The following are typical null hypotheses:

- No difference exists between the experimental and the control program's means. For example, no difference exists between privately and publicly managed school cafeterias.

- No difference exists between the sample's (the survey's participants) mean and the population's mean (the population from which the participants were sampled). For example, no difference exists between the sample of teachers chosen to be interviewed and those who were not chosen.

If no difference in means is found, the terminology used is "We failed to reject the null hypothesis." Do not say "We accepted the null hypothesis." Failing to reject the null suggests that a difference probably does NOT exist between the means, say, between the mean opinion scores in School A versus those in School B. If the null is rejected, then a difference exists between the mean opinion scores. Until the data are examined, however, you do not know if School A is favored or if School B is. All you know from the test is that a difference exists in means.

When you have no reason to suspect in advance which of two scores is better, you use a two-tailed hypothesis test. When you have an alternative hypothesis in mind, say, A is better than B, you use a one-tailed test. The tails in hypothesis testing refer to the extreme ends of a statistical distribution. The idea is that if you obtain a statistic that is way out in one or other tail or end of the expected distribution (according to or derived from the null hypothesis distribution), then you reject the null.

2. *State the level of significance for the statistical test (e.g., the t test) being used.* The level of significance, when chosen before the test is performed, is called the alpha value (denoted by the Greek letter α). The alpha gives the probability of rejecting the null hypothesis when it is actually true. Tradition keeps the alpha value small—.05, .01, or .001—because you do not want to reject a null hypothesis when in fact it is true and there is no difference between group means.

The p value is the probability that a difference as least as large as the obtained difference would have come about if the means were really equal. The p is calculated AFTER the statistical test and is sometimes called the **observed** or **obtained significance level.** If the p value, or observed significance, is less than alpha, then the null is rejected.

Current practice requires the specification of exact or obtained p values. That is, if the obtained p is .03, report that number rather than $p < .05$. Reporting the approximate p was common practice when tables in statistics texts were used to find the **critical values** of a distribution. The critical value is the absolute value that a test statistic must exceed for the null hypothesis to be rejected.

Although the computer output for commercially available programs gives exact ps, the practice of giving approximations (.05, .01, .001) has not been eradicated. The merit of using the exact values is that, without them, a finding of $p = .06$ may be viewed as not significant, whereas a finding of $p = .05$ will be.

3. *Determine the critical value the test statistic must attain to be significant.* Each test statistic, such as the mean, t, F, and chi-square, has a distribution. This distribution is called the **sampling distribution.** Its mean is called the **expected value,** and its variability is called the **standard error.**

All test statistic distributions are divided into an area of rejection and an area of acceptance. With a one-tailed test, the rejection area is *either* the upper or the lower tail of the distribution. For a two-tailed test, you have two areas of rejection: one in each tail of the distribution.

Critical values can be found in statistical tables, and these can be found in statistics textbooks. For example, for the z distribution with an alpha of .05 and a two-tailed test, tabular values will show that the area of acceptance for the null hypothesis is the central 95% of the z distribution and that the areas of rejection are the 2.5% of the area in each tail. The value of z that defines these areas is -1.96 for the lower tail and $+1.96$ for the upper tail. If the test statistic is less than -1.96 or greater than $+1.96$, it will be rejected. The areas of acceptance and rejection in a standard normal distribution, using $\alpha = .05$, is illustrated in Figure 2–3.

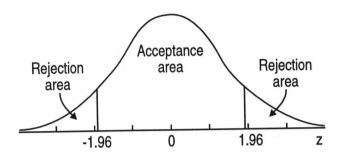

Figure 2–3. Areas of Acceptance and Rejection in a Standard Normal Distribution, Using $\alpha = .05$

4. *Perform the calculation.* Numerous statistical packages are available for making statistical computations. To choose one, read the software reviews in professional journals of education, business, law, statistics, epidemiology, and medicine. Another option is to ask for recommendations. All statistical packages have a manual (and/or tutorial) that teaches how to create data files and give the appropriate commands.

3

Selecting Commonly Used Statistical Methods for Surveys

This chapter provides a guide to the selection of commonly used data-analytic methods. For simplicity, the guide omits ordinal variables. When independent variables are measured on an ordinal scale, they are often treated as if they were nominal. For example, to predict the outcomes of participation in a program for clients with good, fair, and poor emotional health, rather than treating good, fair, and poor as ordinal variables they can be converted to nominal variables: good (yes or no), fair (yes or no), poor (yes or no).

When dependent variables are measured on an ordinal scale, they are habitually treated as if they were numerical. Suppose the dependent variable in a nutrition program is men's and women's ratings of self-esteem (10 = *very high* and 1 = *very low*). The dependent ordinal variable can, for the sake of the analysis, be regarded as numerical, and mean ratings can be computed.

Before conducting any statistical analysis, check the assumptions in a statistics text or computer manual. If the survey data do not meet the assumptions, look for other statistical methods to use. Even if your data appear to meet the assumptions, check once again after the analysis is performed by studying the computer printout. If you are using correlations or regressions, are the assumptions met concerning linearity? If you are using an independent *t* test, are the variances equal?

Following the guide, the chi-square, *t* test, and analysis of variance (ANOVA) are introduced because of their utility in analyzing survey data. The guide also refers to methods for analyzing data that are not discussed in this book. These methods are complex, but they build upon the principles and assumptions included in this overview. Further information about these methods can be obtained from sources listed in the Suggested Readings section at the end of this book.

General Guide to Data-Analytic Methods in Surveys

Sample Survey Objective	Type of Data		Potential Analytic Method
	Independent Variable	Dependent Variable	
For objectives with one independent and one dependent variable:			
To compare experimental and control counties in children's reported use or failure to use bicycle helmets	Nominal: group (experimental and control)	Nominal: use of helmets (used helmets or did not)	Chi-square; Fisher's Exact Test
To compare experimental and control groups in their attitudes (measured by their scores on the Attitude Survey)	Nominal (dichotomous): group (experimental and control)	Numerical (attitude scores)	One sample *t* test, dependent *t* test, and independent samples *t* test; Wilcoxon Signed-Ranks Test; Wilcoxon Rank-Sum Test (the Mann-Whitney *U*)
To compare teens in the United States, Canada, and England with respect to their attitudes (measured by their scores on the Attitude Survey)	Nominal (more than two values): United States, Canada, and England	Numerical (attitude scores)	One-way analysis of variance (uses the *F* test)
To determine if high scores on the Attitude Survey predict high scores on the Knowledge Test	Numerical (attitude scores)	Numerical (knowledge scores)	Regression (when neither variable is independent or dependent, use correlation)
For objectives with two or more independent variables:			
To compare men and women in the experimental and control programs in terms of whether or not they adhered to a diet	Nominal (gender, group)	Nominal (adhered or did not adhere to a diet)	Log-linear

(continued)

51

General Guide to Data-Analytic Methods in Surveys (continued)

Sample Survey Objective	Type of Data — Independent Variable	Type of Data — Dependent Variable	Potential Analytic Method
To compare men and women with differing scores on the Knowledge Test in terms of whether or not they adhered to a diet	Nominal (gender) and numerical (knowledge scores)	Nominal and dichotomous (adhered or did not adhere to a diet)	Logistic regression
To compare men and women in the experimental and control programs with respect to their attitudes (measured by their scores on the Attitude Survey)	Nominal (gender and group)	Numerical (attitude scores)	Analysis of variance (ANOVA)
To determine if age and income and years living in the community related to attitudes (measured by scores on the Attitude Survey)	Numerical (age and income and years living in the community)	Numerical (attitude scores)	Multiple regression
To compare men and women in the experimental and control programs in their attitudes (measured by their scores on the Attitude Survey) when their level of education is controlled	Nominal (gender and group) with confounding factors (such as education)	Numerical (attitude scores)	Analysis of covariance (ANCOVA)

For objectives with two or more independent and dependent variables:

Sample Survey Objective	Type of Data — Independent Variable	Type of Data — Dependent Variable	Potential Analytic Method
To compare men and women in the experimental and control programs in their attitude and knowledge scores	Nominal (gender and group)	Numerical (scores on two measures: attitudes and knowledge)	Multivariate analysis of variance (MANOVA)

Reading Computer Output

Suppose an evaluator needs a chi-square analysis. Depending on the statistical program, the output will contain the analysis and additional information. Computer printouts vary in how they present results and in the additional tests and data they provide. Evaluators should become multilingual in output terms so that they can adequately read and talk about a range of statistical programs. Experience helps, and so, in the next few sections, two commonly used statistical techniques are discussed and their corresponding output in one program application are illustrated.

CHI-SQUARE

The **chi-square** (Greek letter chi, χ^2) distribution is the most commonly used method of comparing proportions.

Suppose you survey 208 high school seniors to find out their career preferences. Of this group, 103 have spent a year in a special job training program; the others have not. The survey finds that 40 seniors prefer to go on to college before seeking employment, whereas the remainder prefer to enter the labor force immediately.

The questions you are interested in answering are these:

1. Does a difference exist between program participants and the others in the number or proportion of seniors preferring to continue their education?

2. Does an association (or relationship) exist between being in the program and also preferring to continue in college?

To answer these questions, you could create a table that looks like this:

	Marginal Frequencies		
	Job Program	No Program	Total
Prefer college			40
Do not prefer college			168
Total	103	105	208

The **marginal frequencies** represent the numbers or proportions of seniors in the two survey groups. The **expected frequencies** shown in the table below represent the numbers or proportions of seniors in each **cell**, assuming that no relationship (the null hypothesis) exists between preference and program participation:

	Expected Frequencies		
	Job Program	No Program	Total
Prefer college	20	20	40
Do not prefer college	84	84	168
Total	104	104	208

The expected frequencies refer to the hypothetical distribution if the views of the two groups being compared are alike. So if 40 people prefer college, as the illustrative survey finds, then the expected frequency is 20 in the Job Program group and 20 in the group of nonparticipants.

Chi-square tests enable you to compare the expected frequency in each cell with the frequency that actually occurs (**observed frequencies**). The observed frequencies refer to the survey's data. The differences between observed and expected frequencies are combined to form the chi-square statistic. If a relationship exists between the column and row variables (e.g., whether or not the person is in a program and his or her preference), the two are said to be dependent. In this case, you would decide in favor of differences between the groups.

To assist you in using chi-square tests with two groups (e.g., experimental and control) and a two-pronged **dichotomous** nominal survey outcome (e.g., yes, prefer college or no, do not prefer college), use the following notation:

	Experimental	Control	Total
Positive	a	b	a + b
Negative	c	d	c + d
Total	a + c	b + d	a + b + c + d = n

This is called a 2 × 2 table. The formula for calculating the chi-square for data in a 2 × 2 table is

$$\chi^2(1) = n(ad - bc)^2/(a + c)(b + d)(a + b)(c + d).$$

The (1) refers to the degrees of freedom, a **parameter** that is used also in the *t* distribution. A parameter is the population (as contrasted with a sample) value of a distribution (e.g., the mean of the population is μ, and the standard deviation is σ). The chi-square test is performed as a one-tailed test. If the observed frequencies depart from the expected frequencies by more than the amount that you can expect by chance, you reject the null.

Going back to the example of preference for college when comparing program and nonprogram participants, suppose the 2 × 2 table was filled out to look like this:

	Jobs Program	No Program	Total
Prefer college	80	30	110
Do not prefer college	23	75	98
Total	103	105	208

Using the formula, you would have the following calculations:

$$\chi^2 (1) = n(ad - bc)^2/(a + c)(b + d)(a + b)(c + d).$$

$$\chi^2 = \frac{208[(80)(75) - (30)(23)]^2}{(103)(105)(110)(98)}$$

$$\chi^2 = \frac{208(5310)^2}{116585700}$$

$$\chi^2 = 50.30.$$

The critical value for an α of .01 is 6.635. In other words, 99% of the distribution is below 6.635. (You cannot possibly memorize all critical values; with experience, you will become familiar with many.) Any obtained value above the critical value enables you to reject the null hypothesis that no difference exists between the program and no-program groups. In the example, the obtained statistic is above the critical value, and so the null is rejected. The conclusion is that differences exist between the groups and preference for college is related to program participation.

Chi-square tests can be performed with many numbers of columns and rows. Sometimes, chi-square values are "corrected" with a **continuity correction** or **Yates's correction.**

The correction involves subtracting 0.5 from the absolute value of ad – bc before squaring. Its purpose is to lower the value of the obtained statistic, reducing the risk of a Type I error (rejecting the null when it is true); however, the risk of a Type II error (failing to reject the null when it is false) increases. Finally, when the expected frequencies are small (less than 5), then **Fisher's Exact Test** can be used (for more about this method, consult the appropriate sources in the Suggested Readings section at the end of this book).

Example 3.1 illustrates how to read chi-square output from one sample program (SPSS/PC+). As you can see, besides the significance of the differences, a number of other statistics are also provided. These will vary in importance according to the complexity of the survey and the computer program you use.

EXAMPLE 3.1
Reading Computer Output: Chi-Square

Concern has been raised that unemployed people in Community A do not have adequate access to health care; because of this, they do not get to see physicians when they need to. Does a difference exist in use of services between people who are employed and those who are unemployed? More specifically, does the proportion of people who have a paying job differ from the proportion who do not in terms of whether or not they have seen any doctor (MD) more than once?

Type of Survey: Self-administered questionnaire

Survey Questions:
- In the past year, did you see any MD more than once? (yes or no)
- In the past year, did you have a full- or part-time paying job that lasted 9 months or more? (yes or no)

Independent Variable: Job status (having a full- or part-time paying job or not having one)

Dependent Variable: Use of health services (seeing an MD more than once)

Analysis Method: Chi-square

Computer Output: (sample)

Page 22   SPSS/PC+   6/24/93

a

Q41C   SEE ANY MD MORE THAN ONCE   by   Q61   PAYING JOB

		Q61		Page 1 of 1
	Count	*c*	*d*	
	Row Pct	YES	NO	
	Col Pct			Row
		1.00°	2.00°	Total
Q41C				
e YES	1.00	224	631	855 *g*
		26.2 *k*	73.8 *k*	67.7
		64.6 *l*	69.0 *l*	
f NO	2.00	123	284	407 *h*
		30.2 *k*	69.8 *k*	32.3
		35.4 *l*	31.0 *l*	
	Column	347 *i*	915 *j*	1262 *m*
	Total	27.5	72.5	100.0

Page 23   SPSS/PC+   *p* 6/24/93

Chi-Square	Value *n*	DF *o*	Significance
q Pearson	2.23778	1	.13467
r Continuity Correction	2.04057	1	.15315
s Likelihood Ratio	2.21574	1	.13661
t Mantel-Haenszel test for linear association	2.23601	1	.13483

u Minimum Expected Frequency - 111.909

Number of Missing Observations: 20

Interpretation (refer to corresponding letters marked on computer printout)

a. Q41c refers to the question on the self-administered questionnaire that asks whether the respondent has seen any MD more than once.

b. Q61 refers to the question on the self-administered questionnaire that asks whether the respondent has a paying job.

c. Yes is the column that refers to the positive answer to the question about having a paying job.

d. No is the column that refers to the negative answer to the question about having a paying job.

e. Yes is the row that pertains to the positive answer to the question pertaining to seeing or not seeing any MD.

f. No is the row that pertains to the negative answer to the question pertaining to seeing or not seeing any MD.

g. Total number (855) and percentage (67.7) of people who saw an MD more than once.

h. Total number (407) and percentage (32.3) of people who did not see an MD more than once.

i. Total number (347) and percentage (27.5) of people who have a paying job.

j. Total number (915) and percentage (72.5) of people who do not have a paying job.

k and l. Percentage of people represented in each cell. For example, in the top left-hand cell (Cell a), there are 224 respondents. They represent 26.2% of the 855 who saw any MD more than once and 64.6% of the 347 who also have a paying job.

m. Total number of respondents (1,262).

n. Value refers to the results of the statistical computation.

o. Degrees of freedom.

p. Obtained p value. This value is compared to alpha. If it is less, the null is rejected.

q. Pearson is the particular type of chi-square statistic calculated by this particular statistical package.

r. Continuity correction involves subtracting .05 from the difference between observed and expected frequencies before squaring to make the chi-square value smaller.

s. The likelihood ratio is the odds that the results occur in respondents who have seen any MD more than once versus those who have not.

t. Mantel-Haenszel Test for linear association is a log-rank test for comparing two survival distributions. [NOTE: if you do not know what this or any other test means, consult the appropriate sources at the end of this book.]

u. Minimum expected frequency will tell if you have enough observations to proceed with the chi-square test or if you should consider Fisher's exact test.

Conclusion: The obtained significance level is .13467. The null hypothesis (no differences exist between respondents with and without paying jobs in whether or not they saw any MD) is retained.

t TEST

The t test's probability distribution is similar to the standard normal distribution, or z. It is used to test hypotheses about means and thus requires numerical data. The shape of a *t* distribution approaches the bell shape of a standard normal distribution, which also has a mean of 0 and a standard deviation of 1, as the sample size and degrees of freedom increase. In fact, when the sample has 30 or more respondents, the two curves are very similar, and either distribution can be used to answer statistical questions. Current practice in most fields, however, relies on the *t* distribution even with large samples.

Three situations can arise in which *t* tests are appropriate, as illustrated in Example 3.2.

EXAMPLE 3.2
Three Situations and the *t* Test

Survey 1: *Children's Birthday Gifts*

Children in McCarthy Elementary School received an average of 4.2 birthday gifts. How does this compare to the results obtained in the national survey of children and birthday gifts?

Type of t: One-sample *t*

Comment: The mean of a group is compared to a **norm,** or standard value (the results of the national survey).

Survey 2: *Low-Fat Diet for Men at the Computer Chip Plant*

Do average scores on the Feel Good Inventory change for the 50 men after they participate in the Low-Fat Diet Program?

Type of t: Dependent *t*

Comment: The mean of a single group is compared at two times (before and after participation in the Low-Fat Diet Program).

Survey 3: Learning the Ballet

On average, how do men and women compare in their attitudes toward ballet after participation in the ballet exercise program? The highest possible score is 50 points.

Type of t: Independent *t*

Comment: The means of two independent groups are compared.

To apply the *t* test appropriately, the survey data must meet certain assumptions. To use the *t* distribution for one mean (as in Survey 1 above), the assumption is that the observations (e.g., scores) are normally distributed. Some computer programs provide a probability plot that will enable you to certify that the data are consistent with this assumption. Sometimes, you can examine the distribution yourself. If the data are not normally distributed, they can be transformed into a normal distribution. Alternatively, you can decide not to use the *t* and instead use different statistical measures called nonparametric procedures to analyze the data. Nonparametric methods make no assumptions about the distribution of observed values.

A paired design is used to detect the difference between the means obtained by the same group, usually measured twice (as in Survey 2 above). With the paired *t*, the assumption is that the observations are distributed normally. If the survey data violate the assumption, a commonly used nonparametric test for the difference between two paired samples is the **Wilcoxon Signed-Ranks Test.** This method tests the hypothesis that the medians, rather than the means, are equal (consult sources at the end of the book for more information on this test).

The *t* test for independent groups (Survey 3 preceding) assumes that the observations are normally distributed and that the variances of the observations are equal. If the sample sizes are equal, unequal variances will not have a major effect on the significance level of the test. If they are not, a downward adjustment of the degrees of freedom is made (you have fewer), and separate variance estimates are used instead of the combined or "pooled" variance. The statistical test to compare variances is the *F* test; many computer programs perform this test, often in the same program that performs the *t* test. If one of the assumptions of the independent *t* test is violated, an alternative is the nonparametric **Wilcoxon Rank-Sum Test (Mann-Whitney U)**. This test assesses the equality of medians rather than means, as does the Wilcoxon Signed-Ranks Test.

Example 3.3 is a sample computer printout for a *t* test from SPSS-PC+.

EXAMPLE 3.3
Reading Computer Output:
Independent Samples *t* Test

County A's health planners are concerned that sicker people may not be using the People's Ambulatory Care (PACE) clinic as often as they should. A survey is conducted to find out if this concern warrants attention.

Type of Survey: Self-administered questionnaire

Survey Questions
- In the past year, did you see any MD more than once? (yes or no)

- The Instrumental Activities of Daily Living (IADL) measure has 20 questions about a person's ability to function and perform various tasks including personal care and home chores. A score of 100 represents maximum functioning.

Independent Variable: Use of health services (seeing an MD more than once at PACE or not)

Dependent Variable: Ability to function (score on the IADL)

Analysis Method: t test

Computer Output: (sample)

- -

Page 97   SPSS/PC+   6/23/93

Independent samples of Q41D - SEE MD AT PACE CLINIC > 1 TIME
                                    a   *b*
Group 1: Q41 EQ   1.00   Group 2: Q41 EQ   2.00

t-test for: IADL

	c Number of Cases	*d* Mean	*e* Standard Deviation	*f* Standard Error
Group 1	561	75.5246	23.957	1.011
Group 2	311	77.4358	24.112	1.367

	Pooled Variance Estimate			Separate Variance Estimate		
g F Value	*h* 2-Tail Prob.	t Value	Degrees of Freedom	2-Tail Prob.	t Value	Degrees of Freedom	2-Tail Prob.
1.01	.890	-1.13	870	.261	-1.12	636.61	.262

- -

Interpretation (refer to corresponding letters marked on computer printout)

a. Group 1 answered yes to the question "Did you see an MD at the PACE clinic more than once this year?" The choices were 1 = yes and 2 = no.

b. Group 2 answered no to the question "Did you see an MD at the PACE clinic more than once this year?"

c. Number of cases refers to the number of respondents (sample size) in each group.

d. Mean score obtained on the IADL by each group.

e. Standard deviation of the scores.

f. Standard error of the means.

g. *F* value or statistic obtained in the test to determine the equality of the variances.

h. Probability of obtaining a result like the *F* value if the null is true. If the obtained probability is less than some agreed-on alpha like .05 or .01, the null is rejected. In this case, the probability of .890 is greater than .05, and so the null is retained. The conclusion is that no differences exist in the variances of the two groups.

i. The pooled variance estimate is used when variances are equal. The *p* value is .261, greater than an alpha of .05. The null hypothesis regarding the equality of the group means is retained.

j. The separate variance estimate is used when variances are not equal.

Conclusion: No differences exist in functioning between respondents who saw a doctor at the PACE clinic more than one time and those who did not.

ANALYSIS OF VARIANCE (ANOVA)

Analysis of variance is commonly abbreviated as ANOVA. You use ANOVA to compare the means of three or more groups. For instance, if you want to compare the mean achievement test scores in reading and math of children in Korea, Japan, and Singapore, you use ANOVA.

With ANOVA you ask the question "Does an *overall* difference exist among the groups?" If the results are significant, you can then ask "Which combinations or pairs are responsible for the difference?"

ANOVA guards against multiple Type I errors. A Type I error occurs when you reject the null, when in fact, no difference exists. If you used *t* tests and an alpha of .05 to compare mean reading scores among children from Singapore, Korea, and Japan, you would need three separate tests: Singapore and Korea, Singapore and Japan, and Japan and Korea.

With three tests, you have a 15% (3% × 5%) chance of incorrectly finding one of the comparisons significant. ANOVA guards against this inflation. It is important to remember, however, that the results of an analysis of variance tell you about the overall or global status of differences among groups. If you find differences, ANOVA does not tell you which groups or pairs of groups are responsible. For that information, you should use post hoc comparisons like Tukey's HSD (honestly significant difference), Scheffé, Neuman-Keuls, or Dunnets procedures. (More information on these techniques can be found in the appropriate sources at the end of the book.)

ANOVA is complex, and whole textbooks have been devoted to it. One-way ANOVAs are used in comparisons involving one factor or independent variable, and two-way ANOVAs are used for two factors. A typical ANOVA table for a one-way analysis of variance is given in Example 3.4.

EXAMPLE 3.4
A Typical ANOVA Table

Source	Degrees of Freedom	Sum of Squares	Mean	F Ratio	p
Between groups					
Within groups					
Total					

ANOVA relies on the F distribution to test the hypothesis that the two variances are equal. The variation is divided into two components: the variation between each subject and the subjects' group mean (e.g., the variation between each participant in the experiment and the experimental group's mean) and the variation between each group mean and the grand mean (the mean of all groups). The sum of squares, mean squares, and degrees of freedom are mathematical terms associated with ANOVA.

Practical Significance:
Using Confidence Intervals

The results of a statistical analysis may be significant but not impressive enough to have practical applications. How can this be? Suppose that after an educational campaign in County A, a 10% increase is reported in the use of bicycle helmets by children. In County B, the control, a 5% increase is reported, and the 5% difference between the two counties is statistically significant. Based on the results, you might be tempted to conclude that the educational campaign is effective. If, however, the expectation was that the campaign was to have reached at least 50% of County A's children, then the 10% achievement level is disappointing. You can conclude that the campaign, although "effective," is too weak to be continued or expanded. With very large samples, even small differences can be significant. When statistical significance alone is inadequate to evaluate survey data, confidence intervals should be used.

Suppose a survey is given to participants of Teach for the World, an international program to encourage the best teachers to participate in the education of children outside their own countries. Because of the complexity of the social and cultural issues involved, eligible teachers are assigned to Program 6, a relatively costly 6-month internship, or to Program 3, which only requires a 3-month internship. Of 800 participants, 480 (60%) respond well to Program 6, and 416 of the 800 (52%) do well in Program 3. Using a chi-square to assess the existence of a real difference between the two treatments, a p value of .001 is obtained. This value is the probability of obtaining by chance the 8-point (60%–52%) difference between teachers in Program 6 and Program 3 or an even larger difference. The point estimate is 8 percentage points, but because of sampling and measurement errors (they always exist), the estimate is probably not identical to the true percentage difference between the two groups of teachers.

A **confidence interval** (CI) provides a plausible range for the true value. A CI is computed from sample data and has a given probability that the unknown true value is located within the interval. Using a standard method, the 95% CI of the 8-percentage-point difference comes out to be between 3% and 13%. A 95% CI means that about 95% of all such intervals would include the unknown true difference and 5% would not. Suppose, however, that given the other costs of Program 6 the smallest practical and thus acceptable difference is 15%, then you can conclude that the 8-point difference between Programs 6 and 3 is not significant from a practical perspective, although it is statistically significant.

The confidence interval and p are related; if the interval contains 0 (no difference), then the p is not significant. However, if much of the interval is above the practical cutoff, then the results can be interpreted as practically inconclusive. For example, if the cutoff were 15% and the CI ranged from –1% to +25%, then much of the interval would fall above the cutoff for practical significance; the survey results would be unclear.

A graphic test for the differences between the means of two independent groups can also be prepared. The 95% CI is calculated and charted. If the means do NOT overlap, differences exist. If the mean of one group is contained in the interval of the second, differences do not exist. If the intervals overlap, but not the means, then you cannot tell if differences exist, and a hypothesis test must be performed. Figure 3–1 shows how charts can reveal differences in independent means.

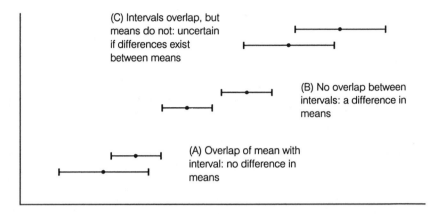

Figure 3–1. Visualizing Differences Between Independent Groups, Using Confidence Intervals

EXERCISE

The following output was obtained from a survey to answer the question, "How do Groups 1, 2, and 3 compare in their attitudes?" A score of 20 was the highest possible; high scores represented the most favorable attitude.

   a. What is the null hypothesis?

   b. Chart the confidence intervals and tell if the differences among the groups are significant.

   c. What is the F probability, and does it agree with the findings you obtained by representing the confidence intervals on a chart?

   d. If you find significance, which of the three groups is likely to have contributed most to the finding?